# Thinking, a diverse and inclusive process

## An epistemological look

*José Manuel Salum Tomé*

Copyright © 2022 José Manuel Salum Tomé
Copyright © 2022 Generis Publishing

All rights reserved. This book or any portion thereof may not be reproduced or used in any manner whatsoever without the written permission of the publisher except for the use of brief quotations in a book review.

Title: Thinking, a diverse and inclusive process

An epistemological look

ISBN: 979-8-88676-168-9

Author: José Manuel Salum Tomé

Cover image: www.pixabay.com

Publisher: Generis Publishing
Online orders: www.generis-publishing.com
Contact email: info@generis-publishing.com

*Inclusive education is the transformation of the system, it highlights difference and diversity, to strengthen the development of skills, under the premise of respect for difference and diversity (Barton L, (2013). Today, educational inclusion is carries out and attends to the educational needs of students individually, where the actors of the educational process contribute to learning while respecting the differences and diversity of each individual, by fulfilling the transforming and integrating role that improves skills and breaks with barriers to learning.*

# Table of Contents

Introduction ..................................................................................... 7
The Epistemology of Education and Diversity ................................. 9
Epistemological Foundations of Inclusive Education and Diversity ................. 10
Philosophy ...................................................................................... 14
thinking and philosophy .................................................................. 14
Epistemology, Thinking and Knowing ............................................ 16
Epistemology ................................................................................... 18
Think Epistemology ........................................................................ 18
Science ............................................................................................ 20
Thinking as a creative act ................................................................ 20
Ontology .......................................................................................... 22
Final reflection ................................................................................ 24
Reference ......................................................................................... 27

# Resume

Contemporary education has taken on the challenge of promoting different programs aimed at promoting inclusive teaching-learning processes that facilitate attention to diversity. It is evident that the integration of students with special needs in regular educational centers has caused significant changes in the curriculum, infrastructure and training among teachers. In the last ten years, educational inclusion has made significant progress, but much remains to be done to expand inclusive spaces.

**Keywords:**

Educational Inclusion - Epistemology - Inclusive classroom - Inclusive teacher

# Introduction

This article carries out an analysis around the main epistemological difficulties that the inclusive education and diversity approach faces today, in public policies of equal opportunities. Initially, it describes a certain epistemic vacuum within the educational sciences and, therefore, an unclear pedagogical knowledge, regarding the foundational dilemmas that it has proposed to solve. A displacement model is observed that advances above the problems of the new century, evidencing a hybrid or preconstructed paradigmatic model or approach, facing the challenges and transformations that postmodern societies demand in times of exclusion. It is concluded about the need to advance towards the assurance of a field of timely curricular, didactic and evaluative problematization in the matter.

# The Epistemology of Education and Diversity

A large percentage of children and adolescents between 5 and 17 years of age are part of school exclusion. In the 60s, 70s and part of the 80s, the genesis of exclusion from education lies in mistreatment, discrimination, neglect of basic physical and emotional needs, among other factors; at that time only normal children received education.

# Epistemological Foundations of Inclusive Education and Diversity

The epistemological foundation of inclusive education at the beginning of the 21st century, opted for a transdisciplinary enrichment that allows promoting a genealogical critique of its founding paradigm of Special Education. Ocampo, (2015) In epistemic terms, inclusive education must address the total eradication of exclusion, that is, it seeks to eliminate school failure and exclusion.

This study presents reflections, to contemporary education, to deal with traditionalist pedagogy, which impede the development of skills, proposes epistemological meditation, which positively contribute to overcoming the conflicts faced by students with special educational needs. .

"Currently, the scenarios in which inclusive education and education for all are promoted have diversified and new subjects and new forms of acceptance and/or social elimination have appeared," Kaplan, (2007) that condition social life and school of multiple students.

An important step is to understand, from an epistemic perspective, that inclusive education is a model or current trend that is different from education for all. Therefore, it is the educational systems and the designers of educational policies who are more aware of what they promote today, because under the model of inclusion, poorly built, new forms of homogenization, marginalization and some contradictions in the management of education become visible. institutions and training practices. The challenge now is that the programs on the matter signify and redefine all our citizens.

Accepting our own history of ways of thinking about the world, we should situate ourselves in what the different narratives and explanations have called the Western tradition of thought, which, in addition to its logical types and rationality, has proposed the paradigm of simplification , this from Plato to classical science has affected philosophy and science, which would not be a major problem if it did not directly impact the field of decision-making, and therefore ethics, aesthetics and politics. Its aim is to *idealize, rationalize, normalize* , that is, conceive of reality as something reducible to schemes or ordered and computer concepts, understood from the perspective of identity logic and the principle of disjunction.

As for ethics and politics, they are also presided over by rationalization and the unifying order, so that they reject or exclude the "less developed" or "irrational" forms. In short, it is a thought that is based on reifying concepts and an epistemological ideal that is characterized by assuming an absolute point of view , that is, an external , omniscient observer . This epistemological conception implies in parallel the idea of an illusory objectivity that is also absolute, which is not affected by the subject/observer. Such an ideal of knowledge, typical of classical philosophy and science, is impossible . From the point of view of action, it is also shown by social and political history, in particular that of our century, which, when it has tried to determine/unify society, has succeeded in the best of cases for a short time.

From the above, we can affirm that our role as educators is to respond to the diversity of the student, the objective of inclusive education, and possibly it is the challenge that the educational system must face, to achieve a quality education that benefits all. students at different levels. The changes proposed in education have caused teachers to feel pressured by the demands regarding the constant curricular overload, updating and professionalization of teachers, among other factors. In order for these pressures to be overcome, it is necessary to promote reforms, both in the cultural, organizational and good practices of schools, in order to achieve a change in the attitude of teachers and thus guarantee access, relevance, participation that facilitates learning. of all students.

Inclusion is a right to education under equal conditions; in this sense, the participation of people is carried out under the slogan of respect for diversity, to contribute to the advancement of society. It is important to be clear that each individual is a different world, and each one has their own learning style, which confirms that they are all different.

All of the above allows us to socialize the term THINKING in our students, it is made clear that everyone has this ability, which is why we will give a perception of *Thinking* from an epitymological perspective.

# Philosophy

## thinking and philosophy

When one hears the word Philosophy, one **thinks** of a person, relaxed, who begins to see and **think** about everything he does and wants to draw conclusions from all actions. It is seen as something dark and mysterious that few men are able to understand and not be able to think about its meaning. However, we see that Philosophy is the most natural activity of man, it is something that comes with his essence. It is simply the curiosity of man for each and every one of his actions and to know how? And for what? is in this world, as person.

Man, because he is not born in the adult stage, gets used to having some questions unanswered and seeing things that he may not understand, but it has always been like that. If man were born an adult, he would ask himself many questions since he would not even know how? why? or what for? is here, therefore the power is restricted To think. Philosophy is the knowledge that human reason claims immediately and naturally, its definition is as follows: **Science of all things by their ultimate causes acquired by the light of reason.**

For its ultimate causes. This speaks of the fact that he studied all the meanings of a subject, not by parts, nor by specialization, but rather everything in general, so that there is a greater understanding. Acquired by the light of reason. This tells us that Philosophy is not based on facts of faith, but on real facts, on questions verifiable to man's reason.

In this sense, we can say that the sciences do not think. This does not mean anything negative; on the contrary, the sciences know much more than **thinking** . They accumulate knowledge about the world that "is there". **Thinking** , on the other hand, does not accumulate knowledge, it only questions the origin of the world. We don't **think** because the memory of our essential historical being was expelled from the beginning of history. We have entered history expelling from memory the original being that opened this history. Due to this forgetfulness, **we are not thinking** . This forgetting of what essentially originates us, this expulsion from memory of the foundation of our essential historical way of being, constitutes a peculiar way that we human beings have of linking ourselves with the history.

# Epistemology, Thinking and Knowing

**Think** and Knowledge. The act of thinking and its results, thoughts are still a complex problem for Philosophy. In fact, to **think** is to know. But **what** is thinking? Plato says that it is to remember. Descartes that is to doubt, affirm, deny, want, not want, imagine, feel. While Hegel affirms that it is the realization for himself of the effective reality of the absolute through human language.

However, diversity, we can characterize **thinking** as a psychological activity, as the act that occurs in the consciousness of a subject in a certain period of time, which can be performed with full attention, distraction, with pleasure or dislike. The result of this activity is the **thought** that as such is indifferent to who thinks it, how and when they think it, maintaining its identity with itself.

In this sense, thought is spaceless and timeless; the Socratic maxim "know yourself", as a thought remains unchanged, regardless of whether it was thought in very particular conditions. Socrates in the 5th century BC, or let me think of it now in a different sense. On the other hand, thought is usually accompanied by perceptions or images, I can see something or imagine it; but these elements are not essential to thought, every time I read a book, I do not imagine everything I am reading. The expression of thought also appears, the signs that express it as its meaning or meaning. Finally, we can point out that the object of thought, the reference. All thought is thought of something. There are no mere, empty thoughts. We must not, however, confuse thought with its object, since objects as such are not modified by thinking about them.

# Epistemology
# Think Epistemology

The human being lives inserted in a determined physical and social environment. Throughout space and time, he has tried to get to know this medium in various ways and using different procedures, each of which has provided him with a concrete explanation of reality. This explanation has nourished the capital of knowledge that has been accumulating. Sometimes, summarily, other times, an explanation has replaced the previous one.

Knowledge is therefore a possibility and a necessity that all societies have developed in one way or another. In our context, in which social work is located, scientific knowledge is the instrument that we have given ourselves to point out the difference between what is true and what is false. No one can doubt the importance of science in our society. Its development is at the base of the organization and of life Social.

We must question its repercussions in all areas of society. Social work, insofar as it is present in a society where science is the dominant criterion in establishing what is true and what is false, has to ask itself about its scientific character or not.

Epistemology will be a means for this. The conception that we have about it would be determined by considering that it consists of an analysis of the conceptual structures of a particular science and of science in general. This analysis is located at a second order level with respect to scientific reflection itself. Its object of work would be determined not by limited space-time entities..., but by the concepts that the specialists of this science handle for its development (Ulysses Moulines, (1988). Epistemology does not want to impose an a priori system, dogmatic, authoritatively dictating what should be knowledge scientific, otherwise study the genesis Y the structure from scientific knowledge, that is, studying scientific production from all its aspects, without forgetting that the concepts used, and science itself, are produced in a specific context, so the relationship between science and society should be analyzed (Mardones and Ursúa , 1982: 41-44)

# Science
# Thinking as a creative act

It doesn't seem like these are good times, it's for philosophical reflection; however, it is urgent that thought be strengthened in these times when scientific and technical development would be capable of putting an end to the evils that the world suffers. It is neither possible nor desirable to return to a pre-scientific world, from which many can be learned. things, but never idealize it; everything that anarchism has already combated since its origins was present in that world: poverty, exploitation, ignorance, prejudice, disease...; All this is possible to eradicate today by delving into the problems thanks to technological progress.

It depends on us to be capable of a renewal of **philosophical thought** that helps to rationalize and humanize societies, as well as to seize the power that is perpetuated in the hands of a few, or, being consistent with the libertarian point of view, to enable that power is diluted in society as a whole, and that hinder the construction of a decent future for everyone.

Today, more than ever, we have the possibility to plan the world we want, we can be capable of being the legitimate owners of our lives, thoughts and our destination. It can be concluded that a "philosophy of science" is necessary, although it is difficult to determine what its real mission would be. Some authors have decided that Philosophy must precede science and provide it with a solid base; others, that what must be achieved is a theory of knowledge, either popular or academic, or a professional language that synthesizes all scientific, technical and practical languages. Habermas, so critical of Marx for subordinating knowledge to the productive forces, considers that the true mission of philosophy is to be critical of science: "Criticize the objectivist self-conception of the sciences, the scientistic concept of science and scientific progress ; it should deal in particular with basic questions of a social-scientific methodology, so that it does not hold back. But it is required, the adequate elaboration of basic concepts for systems from action communicative"; **Habermas (1981),** not denies the science as the productive force, but it only admits it if it is accompanied by science as the emancipatory force.

# Ontology

Nothing is broader than the sum of **thinking and being** . Everything, both real and unreal, both existing and nothing, is located in one of these two areas, and there is no more. To take them into consideration is to encompass everything and there is no room for a broader totality. However, the sum of thinking and being is not a totality, in the sense that there is a genus to which two species belong, respectively thinking and being. be.

It is a totality only in the sense that any "data" belongs to one or another area; it is a merely quantitative totality, and therefore abstract. Next, it will begin to clarify what is the relationship in which **thinking and being are with each other** . They do not intend to go through all the aspects of the matter, but they do touch on the characteristic points. The historical investigation, so important, but so extensive, is left aside, and it is limited to trying to show the outstanding features of the relationship **thinking - being** compatible and required by "metaphysical realism".

I understand by such realism, from a historiographical point of view, the one found mainly in Aristotle and Saint Thomas Aquinas. From a dogmatic point of view, it is that it admits the possibility of metaphysics, that is, of the science of being as such. Of course, within this path there are numerous variants that are incompatible with each other at some points that are not secondary or little ones.

The **"problem" of thinking and being** is exercised by **thinking**. It is a problem for thinking, because being itself does not question thinking. Thinking questions its relationship with being insofar as thinking understands itself as a modality of being, as a particular way of being, and, on the other hand, insofar as thinking is situated on the horizon of thinking the being, that is, to the extent that thinking wants to be thinking being. It is, therefore, a problem initially raised from **thinking and for thinking**. It is the entire thinking, from the outset, that is in question, when it questions itself about being.

# Final reflection

Epistemologically, education is a diverse and complex process that encompasses all human beings, cultures, religions, ideologies, etc... and that allows us to realize that diversity is present in our society.

Although transformational learning is complex, it is possible and necessary, it invites us to reflect on ourselves and on our work as human beings in a world of which we are a part, and on our ability to understand the processes of change and adapt to them creatively, our survival will depend neither more nor less.

Thinking as a normal process of the human being and viewed from different epistemological perspectives, more so in the case of the human and social sciences, also shows that we are facing different epistemological positions. Thinking is a discipline that belongs to this category. There is a clear difficulty in defining its object or objects of study, which causes a proliferation of theories based on diverse philosophical assumptions. Teaching has to think implies making these presuppositions patent. In this way, the different theories can be ordered showing the configuration of the world that they presuppose. Teaching the Thinking process involves influencing the configuration of the students' network of beliefs so that they can place their object of study within the framework of a certain vision of reality.

Epistemology, evidently, is complexity. It is transcomplexity. But, it is authentic rationality. However, all this is better appreciated when it is developed as a work of intellectual craft characterized by the deep desire to know and, to that end, by the yearning to find a type of knowing that, once it becomes conscious, is diluted in new understandings. Because this is another feature of epistemological thinking: to evolve –this concept is applied to oneself-. In addition, it transcends mere grammatical categories, it is transformational and transgressive of all order.

Epistemology overcomes the statements of opportunity and context and is always open to the scenario where the probable, the possible and the uncertain come together, again, in favor of the historical formulation of new knowledge, in direct and proportional relationship with the future. of the science. Without neglecting that epistemology itself takes flight, in such a way that, on occasions, it assumes scientific leadership.

It has been said that epistemology is a *sine qua non condition* for any attempt associated with science, in addition to being a direct access door to philosophical insight.

# Reference

Barton L, L. ((2013). *Inclusive education and teacher education: A foundation of hope or a discourse of delusion.* London: University of London.

CONADIS. ((2013). *National Agenda for Equality in Disabilities.* Quito, Ecuador: CONADIS.

Constitution of the Republic of Ecuador. (20 of 10 of (2008). The Constitution of the Republic of Ecuador Legislative Decree s/n. Montecristi, Manabí, Ecuador: Official Register 449.

Escribano A. and Martínez A. ((2013). *Educational Inclusion and Inclusive Teachers.* Madrid: Narcea Ediciones.

HABERMAS J., (1981). Theorie des kommunikatives Handelns, Frankfurt 1981, volume I, 225 ss

isch. LE (2011). Current proposals and challenges in education: the Ecuadorian case. *Educação & Sociedade, Campinas - Brazil,* , 373-391.

John R, C. (2016). Normal School of Specialization Humberto Ramos Lozano. *National and international journal of inclusive education* , Monterrey. Mexico, p. 264-275.

Ocampo G, A. (2015). *Thesis Epistemology of Inclusive Education.* Granada Spain: University of Granada, p. 152.

OEA, O.d. (2014). *Advances and challenges of inclusive education in Ibero-America.* Buenos Aires: Organization of Ibero-American States.

WHO, . M. (2011). *International classification of functioning, disability and health.* Geneva, Switzerland.

MARDONES, JM and URSÚA, N.: Philosophy of the human and social sciences. Fontamara. Logo Collection. Barcelona, 1982.

NOMADS. (2007). . 27, Pages: 62-73, Central University, Colombia

Santos, M. (DNI: 72097495Q). Epistemology in Education.

UNESCO. (2008). *Inclusive Education, The Way to the Future, Meeting 48 of the International Conference on Education.* Retrieved on September 16, 2018, from http://www.ibe.unesco.org/fileadmin/user_upload/Policy_Dialogue/48th_ICE/Press_Kit/Glyer_ICE_Sp.pdf

www.ingramcontent.com/pod-product-compliance
Lightning Source LLC
Chambersburg PA
CBHW041615220426
43670CB00001B/21